Is Your Glass Half Full?

A Journey of Self-Discovery and a Blueprint for Your Future

TRACY RUSSEK

iUniverse, Inc.
Bloomington

Is Your Glass Half Full?
A Journey of Self-Discovery and a Blueprint for Your Future!

iUniverse books may be ordered through booksellers or by contacting:

iUniverse
1663 Liberty Drive
Bloomington, IN 47403
www.iuniverse.com
1-800-Authors (1-800-288-4677)

ISBN: 978-1-4759-6660-2 (sc)
ISBN: 978-1-4759-6661-9 (hc)
ISBN: 978-1-4759-6662-6 (e)

Library of Congress Control Number: 2012923355

Printed in the United States of America

iUniverse rev. date: 1/3/2013

To my grandson, Devin,

who always keeps my glass full!

Introduction

There is a saying that goes; "If you always do what you've always done, you'll always get what you've always gotten." In other words, if you are not happy or satisfied with your life, nothing will change unless you yourself change it. How we view our lives and how we react to situations and people around us greatly affects our behavior, success, and contentment with life. Look around you at the world in which we live. It seems as though we are constantly bombarded by negative situations such as war, poverty, and disease. When we allow this negativity to permeate our consciousness, it makes being positive about our lives very difficult. We can't change the world, but we *can* change how we view it and how we let it affect our lives. If you view your life in negative terms, you see your glass as *half empty*; however, it is also *half full!*

Everything in life has an opposite. What goes up must come down; things are hot or cold, fast or slow, plain or fancy. Our emotions about life and ourselves also have opposites. We can be happy or sad, feel love or hate, be greedy or generous. Often, without our even knowing it, the opposites of life affect us dramatically. That is why it is so important for us to know our hidden selves.

There are many factors that can affect your life. A few examples include the environment in which you live, your family and friends, and your successes and failures. There are also biological factors that may affect the way you view life. Is there a history of depression in your family? Have you inherited a disease or learning disabilities? Life gives all of us challenges, some more difficult than others. It isn't the severity of the challenges that count, but how we choose to face them. Do we dwell on the negative aspects of our lives and travel down the "woe is me" road? Or do we focus on the positive aspects of life and use the tools we have to make our lives better? Life is a series of choices, and our emotional state plays a major role in helping us make the right choices at the right time.

If we are positive individuals and work toward bettering our lives, we generally make the right decisions. But it is also important for positive people to recognize and acknowledge their opposite side, so as to be prepared for the pitfalls of life and not slip into the negative. It is not humanly possible to be 100 percent positive twenty-four hours a day, 365 days a year. Life will present each of us with situations that will initially spark a negative reaction. However, by being aware that this possibility exists, we can be sure that our reactions will be more positive and prevent the situation from becoming worse.

Those individuals who see life in a negative way definitely need to meet and greet their positive selves. People who constantly see the negativity of life appear to be totally unaware of their positive side. It is so much easier for them to blame their problems on others or on life in general than to recognize the positive direction they can take. By taking the time to see the situation from a positive point of view, they could possibly turn a bad situation into a good one, or at least lessen its negative effect.

The purpose of this book is to guide you through a series of exercises that will help you discover your other self. You will begin by learning about the basic psychology of human behavior. You will become familiar with the research and theories of Ivan Pavlov, Sigmund Freud, Erik Erikson, B. F. Skinner, and Albert Bandura. I have chosen them because their studies are interesting and their theories can be applied to various life situations.

How Will Studying Human Behavior Affect Your Attitude?

It is important for you to have a basic understanding of human behavior in order to explore who you really are and better understand the patterns of behavior in your life. The goal of this self-exploration is to blend your two sides into one. Just as a quarter has two sides but is still one quarter, each person has both positive and negative aspects that come together to create the whole individual. It is my hope that by learning about both sides of yourself, you will become more aware of the choices you make and the behavior you display in your interactions with the world around you.

This is a workbook, and as you go through this book you will be working on improving yourself personally and socially. Therefore, it is very important for you to be completely honest with your responses to the questions and activities presented. Honesty doesn't come easily to us because it means we have to accept our faults. It is easy to acknowledge our positive qualities, but it is not so easy to admit the negative traits that affect our lives. This is your workbook, and no one else should read it but you. Read each section carefully and take time to reflect on your responses.

I hope this book will touch readers of all ages. If you are a younger person, then some of the questions relating to experiences in later life may not apply to you. As you read and consider these questions, focus on where you would like to be at that time of your life and respond accordingly.

May you learn valuable lessons about yourself, realize that you are in control of your life regardless of your age, and learn to make the wisest possible choices. Above all, may you recognize that you are a worthwhile and unique person and that you deserve satisfaction and contentment.

This is your life! Remember, it's not the difficulty of our challenges that counts; how we handle them is what makes life a journey worth taking.

PART I

Understanding Behavior

CHAPTER I

The Beginning

Have you ever taken the time to study your image in a mirror? Have you ever stared into your eyes and asked the question, "Who am I?" If you have, then you know that this can be a very interesting and introspective activity. If you have never studied your image in the mirror, this would be a great time to give it a try. Every day you look at your reflection as you brush your teeth or comb your hair, but do you really take the time to know the person looking back at you? It is said that the eyes are the mirror of the soul, revealing the person who lies deep within us. There are parts of our personality that we don't like to recognize. They are like missing puzzle pieces that prevent us from seeing the entire picture.

The following activity is a great way to help you put the pieces together. Spend some time looking at your image in the mirror. Look into your eyes and at your entire face. View yourself from both a positive and negative approach. Does it feel odd to focus on your image in the mirror? Do you honestly know yourself, or is it awkward to face your reflection? What is your life like at this very moment? Are you where you want to be, or do you desire more but do not know how to reach your goal? Consider these questions, and then on the next page, "This is My Life," write a brief but detailed description of how you currently view yourself and the life you are living. Write down everything you felt or noticed about the real you. Fill up the entire space by using words like *happy, sad, angry, frustrated, generous, kind,* and *capable.* Create a map of yourself, of all that you like and dislike about the person you have observed.

This Is My Life

Write a description of your life the way it is right now.

_____
_____
_____
_____
_____
_____
_____
_____
_____
_____
_____
_____
_____
_____
_____
_____
_____
_____
_____
_____
_____
_____
_____
_____
_____

Chapter 2

What Is Psychology?

By definition, psychology is the systematic, scientific study of behaviors, actions, responses to stimuli, and mental processes. This includes mental activities like planning, thinking, imagining, and dreaming, as well as desires that are not so easily observed. When studying human behavior, psychology has three goals: to explain or understand why people behave in a certain way, to predict how they will behave in the future, and to control behavior.

Additionally, psychology raises the question of "nature vs. nurture." Is it an individual's environment that affects his or her behavior (*nature*), the love and care of the family (*nurture*), or a combination of both? Psychologists have argued over the concept of "nature vs. nurture" for many years.

List two major ways in which your environment (nature) and family (nurture) have affected you, both positively and negatively.

_____
_____
_____
_____

Positively affected by my environment:

_____
_____
_____
_____

Negatively affected by my environment:

_____

_____

_____

_____

Positively affected by my family:

_____

_____

_____

_____

Negatively affected by my family:

_____

_____

_____

_____

Biological factors like genes, hormones, and the nervous system interact with our environment to influence learning, personality, memory, motivation, emotions, and coping techniques. For example, learning disabilities can be genetically transferred to an individual, making it more difficult to learn. How this person copes with this disability greatly affects his or her motivation and desire to learn. It also affects his or her self-image (how a person feels about himself or herself), which directly relates to the emotional well-being and personality of the individual. The psychological approach to the resulting behavior is called _biopsychology_. _Bio_ refers to the biological or physical body, and _psychology_ refers to the mind.

Example of biological factors positively affecting an individual: You inherited beautiful blue eyes and receive many compliments from your friends. The compliments make you feel good about yourself, and you're more comfortable in a social situation.

Example of biological factors negatively affecting an individual: You have inherited curly hair, and when it gets wet, it looks awful. Consequently, when you and your friends go to the beach, you never go into the water.

Although you love to swim, you would be embarrassed to have your hair look awful while you're out socially with your friends.

Consider your own physical features and how they may have affected you in a positive or negative way. Write the two most memorable situations below.

Biological factors that positively affect me in social situations:

_____

_____

_____

_____

Biological factors that negatively affect me in social situations:

_____

_____

_____

_____

The *psychoanalytic* perspective is another approach. It focuses on how the stresses of unconscious fears and desires affect behavior and personality.

A positive example of the psychoanalytic approach: As far back as you can remember you've always wanted to be a doctor. This desire has motivated you to study hard and do well in school. Encouraged by your family, you attend medical school and become a successful physician.

A negative example of the psychoanalytic approach: As far back as you can remember you have always been afraid to be alone. This fear has prevented you from being comfortable at home when no one else is there. You are unhappy in your marriage because you married someone in order to not be alone rather than because you really wanted to be with him or her.

Consider your own desires and fears and how they may have shaped your personality. Write the two most memorable situations below.

The positive desires that have affected my behavior and personality are:

_____

_____

_____

_____

The negative fears that have affected my behavior and personality are:

_____

_____

_____

_____

Biopsychology and psychoanalysis are only two of the many psychological approaches that have been developed by psychologists over the years. There are as many different theories and perspectives as there are psychologists. Some psychologists tend to agree with each other while others seem to be in total disagreement and have developed therapies based on their own perspectives of motivation and behavior. As we review the following well-known psychologists and their theories, you should be able to observe the similarities and differences in their psychological approaches.

CHAPTER 3

Learning from the Masters

Before we get into the various theories of Pavlov, Freud, Skinner, Erikson, and Bandura, I would like you to explore the three major goals of psychology from a personal point of view. As you read each goal, think of how it applies specifically to you. In the space provided below each goal, indicate how it might benefit your personal life goals. Please be specific in your responses.

Goal of Psychology #1
To explain or understand why people behave in a certain way:

_____

_____

_____

_____

Goal of Psychology #2
To predict how people will behave in the future:

_____

_____

_____

_____

**Goal of Psychology #3
To control behavior:**

_____

_____

_____

_____

IVAN PAVLOV (1849–1936)

Pavlov's theory is known as classical conditioning. His original interest was in physiology (the study of the body), not psychology (the study of the mind and behavior). He gained fame through his research on digestion.

While studying the digestion of dogs, Pavlov realized there was a direct connection between salivating (mouthwatering) and the digestion that was taking place in the stomach. He discovered that the saliva told the stomach to get ready to digest food. Taking this one step further, Pavlov devised an experiment to determine if this process could be affected by external stimuli (causes). This experiment made Pavlov famous throughout the world.

Classical conditioning involves four main factors known as _unconditioned stimulus, unconditioned response, conditioned stimulus_, and _conditioned response_. In classical conditioning, the stimulus always precedes the response—which, whether conditioned or unconditioned, is always involuntary. The stimulus causes the response without any voluntary participation or behavior.

Pavlov's experiment involved the following steps:

1. The dog saw the food and salivated.
2. Pavlov rang a bell whenever he put food in the dog's mouth.
3. He continued to ring the bell whenever the dog was fed.
4. Eventually, the dog would salivate just with the ringing of the bell.

Although this experiment used dogs as subjects, people can exhibit the same characteristic behaviors.

Positive example of an unconditioned stimulus/response: You hear a group of people laughing and you don't know what is causing their laughter, but hearing it makes you want to laugh as well. The contagious laughter of the people around you (unconditioned stimulus) causes you to laugh along with them (unconditioned response), even though you don't know why you're laughing. The laughter is a positive unconditioned response and makes you feel good.

Negative example of an unconditioned stimulus/response: You are peeling onions and your eyes start tearing. No matter how hard you try, you can't control the tears. The strength of the onions (unconditioned stimulus) caused your eyes to tear (unconditioned response). The tears are a negative unconditioned response, and you are anxious to get the onion-peeling completed.

Can you think of other unconditioned stimuli/responses that you have experienced? Keep in mind that neither the stimulus nor the response can be controlled, and that they can be negative or positive.

I experienced a positive uncontrolled stimulus/response when:

_____

_____

_____

_____

I experienced a negative uncontrolled stimulus/response when:

_____

_____

_____

_____

Conditioned Stimulus: The pairing of one stimulus (food) with another (bell.) *Conditioned Response:* A response that is the result of the conditioned stimulus.

Positive example of a conditioned stimulus/response: Sally and Joyce have been friends for many years, and thanks to their recent busy schedules, it has become increasingly difficult for them to get together socially. They work close to each other, so Sally and Joyce decide to meet for lunch as often as possible. In this example, a conditioned reflex is being paired with Sally and Joyce enjoying a conversation (stimulus) and lunch/food (another stimulus). After a few weeks pass, both ladies discover that whenever they talk on the phone, they start to feel hungry even if they just had food. What has developed over this period of time is a conditioned response where a conversation between them (stimulus) causes them to be hungry (response).

Negative example of a conditioned stimulus/response: A soldier who returns from battle experiences a fight-or-flight reaction (response) to the sound of a firecracker or car backfire (stimulus).

Note: Pavlov discovered that once the stimulus was removed for a period of time, there would no longer be a response.

The concept of stimulus and response is one of the ways we have learned many of our behaviors. What behaviors in your life, both negative and positive, can you attribute to Pavlov's theory?

I experienced a positive conditioned stimulus/response when:

_____

_____

_____

_____

I experienced a negative conditioned stimulus/response when:

_____

_____

_____

_____

SIGMUND FREUD (1856–1939)

Sigmund Freud's theory is called the *psychodynamic theory of personality*. It is based on the fact that an individual's personality is greatly affected by experiences in early childhood that create conflicts between the conscious and unconscious mind. According to Freud, our personality is made up of three parts: the id, the ego, and the superego. If these are not in balance, individuals psychologically protect themselves by using specific defense mechanisms.

The Id: The id's goal is to satisfy biological needs and pursue pleasure. It is the first part of the personality to develop, and it is made up of two biological drives—sex and aggression.

The Ego: The goal of the ego is to find a safe and socially accepted way of satisfying the desires of the id and to negotiate between the id's desires and the superego's values. The ego is the second part of the personality, and it develops from the id during infancy.

The Superego: The superego's goal is to use the morals and values taught by parents or guardians to satisfy a person's wishes and desires in a socially accepted way. It is the third part of the personality and develops from the ego during early childhood.

The id, ego, and superego are like a tennis game. The id and superego are the players and the ego is the tennis ball.

Here is an example of how the game is played: The id says, "I really want those tennis shoes, but I don't have the money to buy them. No one is looking. I think I can put them on my feet and walk out of the store without being caught." The superego replies, "No, you can't do that! It's stealing! If you get caught, your parents will be very upset and disappointed with you! Save up the money, and then buy the shoes." Id replies, "But I can spend the money on something else I want. I know I won't get caught." Superego replies, "But what if you do? Do you really think it's worth getting in trouble?" The id and superego do not talk directly with each other; instead, it is the ego that carries the messages between them in an effort to find a middle ground and come to a safe and socially accepted solution.

Once again, we are looking at opposite forces. The id wants what it wants and doesn't care about the consequences. In this case, it is a negative choice that can result in getting caught stealing. Alternately, the superego wants to take the positive, safe route and save the money to buy the shoes. The ego is placed in the middle, battling between the two and trying to convince the individual to make the right choice.

If we understand how our personality operates, the next time we are placed in a situation where we have to make a decision, we can carefully weigh our options and make the best possible choice toward resolution. Whether it is an important decision or one that requires attention but not to a serious extent, we are constantly faced with situations that require us to make a choice.

Take a few minutes to think about a few memorable times when your id and superego were in conflict with each other and your ego tried to find a solution to the problem. In the space provided below, pick one positive situation and describe it in detail. How were you able to resolve the situation so that a positive choice was made?

Now do the opposite and pick a situation where the choice you made had a negative effect on your life. Why did you make a negative choice, and what was the negative result? If you had the opportunity to have a "do-over," how could you have handled the situation that would have resulted in a more positive outcome for you?

A situation in my life where my id and superego were in conflict and a positive outcome resulted is:

_____

_____

_____

_____

My ego's interaction negotiated a positive result, and I chose to:

_____

_____

_____

_____

A situation in my life where my id and superego were in conflict and a negative outcome resulted is:

_____

_____

_____

_____

My ego's interaction negotiated a negative result, and I chose to:

_____

_____

_____

_____

In this negative situation, if I had taken the time to weigh my options carefully, the positive result could have been:

_____

_____

_____

_____

Often, the poor choices we make are the result of our being egocentric. We are self-centered and observe the situation only from our point of view, and we don't consider the opinions of others and how our choice may negatively affect everyone involved. The ego is not always the "good guy," which is why all aspects of a situation should be considered before making a decision. Recall a time when you found yourself in a similar situation where not only you but also someone else paid the negative consequences. If you had taken the time to listen to the other individual and weigh the options, could the situation have been resolved in a positive way?

A time when my egocentricity caused a problem between me and another person, resulting in a negative outcome, was:

_____

_____

_____

_____

If I had taken the time to listen to the other person's opinion, the problem may have been resolved in a positive way by:

_____

_____

_____

_____

Teenagers often experience periods where they are preoccupied with the way they look, think, and feel, and believe that they will live forever. Peer pressure is extreme, and they want to belong. Freud calls this *adolescent egotism*, a time when your ego puts you in danger because a negative outcome is the result of your being preoccupied with your own desires.

Thousands of teenagers have died because of their desire to belong, and from peer pressure forcing their ego to make poor choices. The best example of this is teenagers drinking and driving. I am sure their parents were diligent in warning them that a serious accident can result from the driver being intoxicated, but as stated above, teenagers have this belief that they have a long life ahead of them and bad things only happen to other kids. It is important for adults to also recognize the pitfalls of adolescent egotism so they can guide young people toward positive choices as serious situations arise.

Whether you are a teenager or an adult, I am sure you have experienced a time when your adolescent ego put you in danger. Take a few minutes to recall the situation and then write it out in detail below. Consider why you took the negative path and what resulted because of your poor choices.

The situation that put me and/or others in danger was:

_____

_____

I made this choice because:

_____

_____

_____

_____

How could the outcome have been positive if I chose to weigh my options carefully and didn't let my ego into the equation?

_____

_____

_____

_____

During the adolescent years, many changes are taking place biologically and emotionally. Hormones are raging, bodies are changing, and teenagers can feel confused and uncertain about what is best for them. If you are young and going through these experiences now, it is important that you confide in one or both of your parents, or find a mentor you trust to discuss your feelings and confusion with. Having the positive support from a trusted adult will help you make good choices.

If you are an adult and have the opportunity to advise a teenager, consider all the positive ways you can guide this young person and create a binding trust so that he or she feels comfortable coming to you for guidance without criticism.

Defense Mechanisms

The ego does everything it can to keep a positive balance between the demands of the id and the superego. However, when life becomes too complicated, the ego needs help. When this happens, the ego unconsciously changes the situation from one that's too complicated to one that is easier to accept—one that will feel less threatening. What the ego does is use techniques that Freud calls *defense mechanisms.* The following are a few of the more familiar and widely accepted techniques.

Denial occurs when a situation becomes too stressful for a person to handle; he or she simply refuses to experience it. *Example:* A child is watching a cartoon when a commercial for a horror movie suddenly comes on. Being a good parent, her father decides to talk with her about it, hoping to alleviate any fear she may have experienced. When her father says, "That commercial was really scary, wasn't it?" the child replies, "What commercial?"

Give an example of a time when you may have used denial:

_____

_____

_____

_____

Repression is not being able to recall a threatening situation, person, or event. *Example:* Whenever Michael misbehaved as a young child, his mother would lock him in his small, dark bedroom closet as a punishment.

Michael has chosen to repress these terrible experiences and no longer consciously remembers them. However, as an adult, he has a very hard time being in small, dark places and prefers to sleep with a night-light on.

If you can remember, describe a time when you may have repressed the memory of a threatening situation. What made you remember it? If you don't remember or never have had this type of experience, can you think of another example?

_____

_____

_____

_____

Displacement results in the redirecting of an impulse as a means of retaliation, because the person you really want to attack is too threatening to you. Instead of facing the person who threatens you, you blame yourself or someone else who is less threatening. *Example:* Remember Michael, who has repressed his experiences of being locked in a closet by his mother? Even though he doesn't remember these experiences, he unconsciously has a valid reason to hate his mother. But hating his mother is too painful for Michael, so instead he directs this hatred toward women in general.

The experience doesn't always have to be repressed for an individual to use displacement. If a child is constantly being bullied by bigger boys at school, rather than face them or report them to an adult, he may bully his younger brother instead.

If you have had a similar experience to one of those above, describe it in detail in the space below. If you can't recall a similar experience, can you think of another example?

_____

_____

_____

_____

Turning against the self occurs when individuals use themselves as a substitute target because the real target is too threatening to them. The individuals involved in this type of situation usually experience negative emotions, such as hatred, anger, and aggression. Freud uses this as an explanation for feelings of inferiority, guilt, and depression. According to many psychologists, refusing to acknowledge one's negative emotions could result in depression. *Example:* A mother discovers that her five-year-old daughter spilled an entire glass of chocolate milk in the living room. She is not feeling well and, without thinking, she negatively lashes out verbally at the child. The child, hurt by the comments of her mother, starts hitting herself. In reality, she would rather be hitting her mother.

Does this remind you of a personal situation, or can you think of another example?

_____

_____

_____

_____

Projection is the tendency to see your own unacceptable desires or negative qualities in other people, and it is amazing how much this defense mechanism is used. *Example:* A loving and faithful husband suddenly becomes attracted to the young and beautiful new secretary at work. Rather than admitting his feelings to himself, he becomes suspicious of his wife.

Describe a time when you may have unconsciously projected your feelings onto someone else. Think hard! We all have used this defense mechanism from time to time.

_____

_____

_____

_____

Undoing is the "magical" way in which unpleasant thoughts or feelings are supposedly canceled after they have already occurred. *Example:* An alcoholic father verbally and physically abuses his children. When Christmas comes around, he buys them expensive gifts in the hopes that the gifts will make up for the abuse. The children, being the target of his abuse, reject the gifts.

The mechanism of undoing isn't always the result of a negative situation. Recently we spent a week in Hilton Head, South Carolina, vacationing with my eight-year-old grandson, Devin. One day we decided to visit Charleston, thinking it was only an hour away. Unfortunately, it was more like two and a half hours, and when we got to our destination, we were all very ready to get out of the car. Although during the trip, Devin was very bored and tired, he behaved extremely well. Because we didn't want the memory of this driving fiasco to spoil his vacation, we rewarded Devin's positive behavior by buying him a souvenir. In this situation, the mechanism of undoing was used in a positive way.

Can you add to the examples above with one of your own?

_____

_____

_____

_____

Regression occurs when an individual is faced with a stressful situation and returns to a psychological time in his or her life when there was less stress. When we are troubled or frightened, our behaviors often become more childish. *Example:* A potty-trained two-year-old starts wetting his bed after his new baby sister is brought home. This is a very common situation, and often the two-year-old regresses to the point of needing to wear a diaper again. His childish behavior will change with parental understanding and an equal amount of attention. The bedwetting may stop if the older child is included in the care and attention given to the infant.

We have all regressed at one time or another under a stressful situation. When has this happened to you?

_____

_____

_____

_____

Rationalization is the way we distort the facts to ourselves to make a situation less threatening. We do this often on a fairly conscious level each time we try to excuse ourselves from a difficult situation. Some people rationalize so often, they begin to believe their own lies to themselves. *Example:* A student is late to class because he was talking with his friends instead of going directly there. He knows he will get a detention for being late, so he tells the teacher he had a bad stomach ache and was in the bathroom. He rationalizes lying to the teacher, which he knows is wrong and therefore threatening, by convincing himself that it is okay because socializing is part of growing up and shouldn't endanger his good record at school.

Have you ever rationalized a situation? If you are human, you have rationalized something you did in your life. Write it in the space below!

_____

_____

_____

_____

Sublimation is when a person channels an unacceptable behavior or impulse into one that is productive and socially acceptable. *Examples:* Someone with a great deal of hostility may become a hunter, a football player, a butcher, or a soldier. Also, a hyperactive individual chooses a profession where he can be mobile rather than one that requires him to sit behind a desk.

Have you ever experienced channeling one of your unacceptable behaviors (we all have them) into an acceptable and productive one? Be honest and remember only you will be reading your responses.

_____

_____

_____

_____

ERIK ERIKSON (1902–1994)

Erik Erikson's concept of human development is called the *psychosexual theory.* According to Erikson, humans continue to develop from the beginning of conception until their death, and childhood is the most important time in their lives. Individuals go through eight stages of life, and their personalities are affected by the experiences they have during each stage. All the stages are within each individual at the time of birth, even though he or she is not aware of them. It is through learned values and family upbringing that the stages unfold, one by one. The eight stages of life are like building blocks; one must be experienced before the next can present itself.

Erikson agreed with Freud's theory of the id, ego, and superego, but felt the ego was the most important and could function separately from the id and superego. According to Erikson's theory, good mental health depends upon whether the ego adjusts positively or negatively to a particular situation.

Let's journey through Erikson's eight stages of human development and, along the way, notice how each stage can have a positive or negative result. By this time, you should know the drill.

First Year of Life: Trust vs. Mistrust

The infant will develop a sense of trust if his or her parents, family, and environment satisfy the basic physical and emotional needs necessary for creating a feeling of trust. On the other hand, if the basic needs of an infant are not met and this trust is not established, the infant will enter the next stage mistrusting the people in his or her life.

Positive example: Johnny is a one-year-old who has just fallen and hit his head on the coffee table. He starts to cry, and within seconds, his mother picks him up, holds him tightly, and whispers soothing words of comfort to him. After he has calmed down, she tends to the small bump on his head. If Johnny's parents continue to support his feeling of trust through this stage of infancy, he most likely will grow up to trust himself and others.

Negative example: Johnny wakes up from his nap with a soiled diaper. He is dirty, wet, and very uncomfortable. He cries, hoping his mother will come to his rescue and change his diaper. However, Johnny's mother is so engrossed in a television program that she is not paying attention to his crying and does nothing to comfort him. Johnny continues crying until he cries himself back to sleep, with his diaper still dirty, wet, and uncomfortable. If this lack of attention by Johnny's mother occurs on a routine basis, Johnny will probably grow up to distrust not only his mother but himself as well.

I learned to trust or mistrust when:

_____

_____

_____

_____

Early Childhood, Ages One to Three:
Autonomy vs. Shame and Doubt

During this stage, a child struggles between self-confidence and self-doubt while attempting to develop independence through experimenting and exploring his or her environment. The child will have a healthy sense of self-confidence if the parents are supportive and encourage his independence (autonomy). The opposite of this is when one or both parents, out of fear that their child may get hurt exploring, create an environment of dependency. This dependency can create a sense of self-doubt in the child, making it more difficult for him or her to be successful in a world that often requires taking chances.

Positive example: Mary is a two-year-old who likes to dress herself, but when she does she mixes up colors, wears clothes backward, and often looks as though she doesn't have many clothes to wear. Mary's mother does not correct her clothing mistakes because she believes it is important for Mary to feel confident about the way she looks and enjoy the independence of choosing her own clothes. Mary may never grow up to become a fashion expert, but she certainly will grow up to feel confident in herself regardless of the clothes she wears.

Negative example: Joey's parents are constantly anticipating his needs and never give him the chance to ask for something. Joey is almost three years old, he has limited speech and poor vocabulary for a three-year-old. If Joey does not have a clinical reason for slower speech development, it may be caused by the lack of a need to communicate.

I learned self-confidence or self-doubt when:

_____

_____

_____

_____

Preschool, Ages Three to Six:
Initiative vs. Guilt

Children will develop a feeling of accomplishment and initiative (drive) if they are given an opportunity to choose meaningful activities. They tend to become leaders, making wise decisions and completing projects. Children who are not given the opportunity to make meaningful choices tend to feel guilty about taking charge of a situation (initiative). They tend to become followers and let others make decisions for them.

Positive example: Marty, who just turned four, has had a birthday party. He seems to be more interested in the boxes that contained his presents than the gifts that were inside. Marty's mother doesn't make a big deal out of the situation. She simply allows Marty to explore and create.

Negative example: Six-year-old Sally has made Christmas decorations and gives them to her mother to put on the tree. They are not very attractive, and instead of showing enthusiasm and hanging the decorations, Sally's mother throws them away. When Sally sees the decorations in the trash, she goes to her room and cries.

Most of us can remember events that happened to us around age six. Can you recall whether or not your parents allowed you to choose your own activities? Do you tend to be a leader or are you more comfortable letting others make the decisions? Wherever your tendencies lie, can you connect them to a time when you were in this period of development?

_____

_____

_____

_____

School Years, Ages Six to Twelve:
Industry vs. Inferiority

At this age, children need to develop a more thorough understanding of the world and how they fit into it. They need to learn the basic social skills necessary for success in school. If children are to be successful, they must develop a sense of industry that enables them to set and attain personal goals. These are the children who have learned to be independent and have been given the positive reinforcement to develop a sense of good self-esteem. However, children who have been made to feel dependent on their parents often develop a feeling of inadequacy that greatly affects their ability to learn and interact with other children.

Positive example: Susie is six years old and starting first grade. During the past six years, her parents have bought her plenty of books, crayons, puzzles and other educational toys. She went to preschool and plays a lot with the other children in the neighborhood. Her parents have encouraged her independence and prepared her for school. She can write her name, knows the numbers from one to twenty, and can say her ABCs. On the first day of school, Sally makes friends and feels very comfortable in her new environment away from home.

Negative example: Joey has rarely been away from his parents during the first six years of his life. Now he has to go to school, and of course, his mother cannot go with him. He is terrified of kindergarten and feels abandoned and lonely. It takes a long time for Joey to make friends.

How did you feel when you started kindergarten? Was this an easy time for you, or did you struggle like Joey? What prior situations caused you to have this feeling?

_____

_____

_____

_____

Adolescence, Ages Thirteen to Eighteen: Identity vs. Role Confusion

A teenager is neither a child nor an adult. This uncertainty can make this stage of life very confusing and often difficult. It is a time of transition, testing limits, and breaking away from parental ties. If teens receive the positive support of their parents and teachers, it is almost assured they will be successful in establishing a good sense of self.

It is also almost certain that if teens are not positively supported by the adults around them, they will be unsuccessful at developing their own independence, their role in life becomes confused, and they have nothing on which to base their identity. This is often referred to as having an identity crisis.

Positive example: Seventeen-year-old Rodney is out with two friends, one of whom is driving. They stop at a party where both friends get drunk, and the driver wants to drive home while intoxicated. Rodney tries to take the keys away without success. The two friends get in the car, but Rodney refuses and calls his dad to come get him. Rodney isn't afraid to call his parents because they have already agreed that if he couldn't drive or be driven because of alcohol use, they would pick him up without any questions being asked.

Negative example: Frank is out with his friends. They go to a rave even though they know their parents forbid it. Frank really doesn't want to go, but he does anyway because he doesn't want his friends to think he's weird. When it's time to go home, Frank and his friends are wasted but get in the car anyway. On the way home, they have a serious accident. The sad part is that even though Frank has gone through this experience, he probably will repeat the same mistake in the future, unless he can find a way to improve his self-esteem.

What is your perspective with regard to both of these examples, and can you relate to either of them?

_____

_____

_____

_____

**Young Adulthood, Ages Nineteen to Thirty-Five:
Intimacy vs. Isolation**

At this time of life, individuals start to develop intimate relationships. An emotionally healthy individual with good self-esteem is generally able to achieve intimacy and has a very good chance of having a healthy relationship.

Positive example: John, who is eighteen, is an attractive guy but not what someone would call downright gorgeous. Throughout his life, John's parents have been very supportive, and because of this, he has developed a great sense of self-esteem. John fits in with all students and has a wonderful girlfriend who he respects and who respects him in return. Although they have been dating for a few months, John and his girlfriend decide to wait until they are both sure their relationship is strong enough before engaging in sex.

Negative example: Both of Linda's parents are alcoholics and have been alcoholics since before she was born. Linda, a twenty-year-old woman, exhibits almost no common physical problems consistent with fetal alcohol effects or alcohol-related neurodevelopmental disorder. Even though she is a beautiful woman, she has a very low opinion of herself. As a young child, she was often left to care for herself, and consequently she never developed a feeling of safety and security in her family. Since she has been dating, Linda has had many boyfriends and will go out with anyone who is willing to spend time with her. If sex is required to have a relationship, then Linda will go along with it, as long as she has someone in her life. Although she appears to have many men in her life, Linda simply cannot find true love and a lasting relationship. Because of her intense need to be loved at any cost, she has created a situation where she is alone in the presence of many.

Depending on your age, how do you feel about these examples? If it applies, was your first intimate experience positive or negative, and what do you feel made it this way?

_____
_____
_____
_____

Middle Age, Thirty-Five to Sixty:
Generativity vs. Stagnation

Generativity means contributing to the next generation. This is a time in people's lives when they need to go beyond their own needs and think of how they can contribute to helping the next generation. It is a time for them to balance out the differences between their dreams and their actual accomplishments. Success during this time of life leaves a person feeling productive, accomplished, and successful.

Alternatively, an individual who seems to be unsuccessful in every endeavor he or she tries will ultimately feel like a failure in life. If a person remains selfish and self-centered, his or her life can lead to a feeling of psychological stagnation.

Positive example: Bob is thirty-five years old and has a very good position with CBS News. It seems like all his life, Bob has wanted to be a reporter, and he was the editor of his high-school newspaper for the four years he attended. Although it was a financial struggle, Bob managed to attend college and earn a bachelor's degree in journalism and a master's degree in communications. Bob is proud to be called a factual, honest, and ethical reporter.

Negative example: David comes from a very wealthy family and has always been given everything he wants. During his early twenties, he attended two universities that both kicked him out. At thirty-eight, David still does not have a college degree and is still living at home in the guesthouse of his parents' estate. His father has given him some menial position in his company, hoping that David will eventually mature and be able to do something with his life. Although David has all the money in the world, unless he makes drastic changes in his life, he will never acquire a sense of accomplishment and self-satisfaction and will probably go through life unhappy, unfilled, and psychologically stagnant.

If your age falls into or is beyond this age, do you relate more to the positive or negative example? Explain why.

_____
_____
_____
_____

If you are younger than this age range, where would you like to be at this time in your life? Explain why.

_____
_____
_____
_____

Later Life, Over Age Sixty-One:
Integrity vs. Despair

At this age, most individuals want to look back on their life with little regret and a feeling that their life has been worthwhile. One who accomplishes this is said to have *ego integrity*.

Unfortunately, others look back on their lives with many regrets and few, if any, accomplishments. They generally end up with feelings of despair, hopelessness, guilt, resentment, and self-rejection. They wonder why they were ever born.

Positive example: Sixty-five-year-old Susan is a retired lawyer who has spent most of her adult life trying to help people with serious legal problems. She was a civil lawyer and, during her practice, acquired a reputation for being honest and ethical. Susan is a healthy and active person, and although she loves the law, she just doesn't want to put in the time required to continue her practice. She is unwilling to just sit around unproductive, however, so she has volunteered at the local business college to use her legal experience to help young entrepreneurs.

Negative example: Remember David? Well, he never did anything but take from his parents, and when both his parents died, David inherited the family estate and fortune. Not so awful, some people would say, but David never did marry, he has no family, and the friends he does have are only his friends because he is so wealthy. At seventy, David lives alone in a big mansion with only servants to keep him company. As he looks back over his life, he sees what a waste he has made of it. He has become a bitter, angry, and miserable old man.

Have you reached this time in your life? If yes, are you looking back at what you have accomplished in life in a positive light or a negative one? Keep in mind there may be a combination of both, since our experience in life cannot be placed in only one category. Additionally, if you feel you wasted your life, don't despair. As long as you are on this earth, you can *always* improve your life by appreciating all the positive things you have accomplished and releasing all the negative things in your life you may wish you never did. Use the space below to express your feelings.

_____
_____
_____
_____
_____
_____
_____
_____
_____
_____
_____

If you are younger than sixty and if you continue on your current path, will you reach this point in your life feeling fulfilled, or do you think your current path will lead to despair? How can you assure yourself a life of satisfaction and contentment?

_____
_____
_____
_____
_____
_____
_____
_____
_____
_____

B. F. Skinner (1904–1990)

Skinner's theory is called *operant conditioning* (stimulus/response). According to this theory, behavior is affected by events (stimuli) that occur in the environment. Response brings about a result. When the stimulus response is reinforced (rewarded), a conditioned response occurs. Once an individual has been frequently conditioned (reinforced) to a stimulus/ response, the need for the stimulus ceases to exist.

Positive example: You are in an elevator with the most attractive person you have ever seen. You kiss that person and he or she kisses you back. This is positive reinforcement. The consequence of your response is positive; therefore, the behavior is reinforced.

Another example: The person on the elevator slaps you until you kiss him or her. This is negative reinforcement. However, the consequence of your response is positive (the termination of a negative stimulus); therefore, the response is reinforced.

Negative example: You are in an elevator with the most attractive person you have ever seen. You kiss the person and he or she slaps you. This is punishment. The consequence of your response is negative; therefore, the response is punished.

What behavior did you learn through operant conditioning? Were you positively or negatively rewarded?

A behavior I could have learned through operant conditioning is:

_____

_____

_____

_____

I learned this behavior through a negative/positive reward because:

_____

_____

_____

_____

Positive Operant Conditioning is the learning that occurs because rewards have affected a behavior to such a degree that the behavior will continue to increase until it becomes an integral part of the individual's personality.

Negative Operant Conditioning is the learning that occurs because consequences have affected a behavior to such a degree that the behavior will cease to exist or will be dramatically reduced.

When a desired response is increased by praise or a feeling of accomplishment, the behavior is positively reinforced. When an unpleasant consequence to an inappropriate negative behavior occurs, resulting in a reduction of that behavior, punishment has occurred. If the punishment is not negatively reinforced (being consistent), the inappropriate behavior will most likely reoccur and possibly increase.

Motivation is the use of either physiological or psychological actions that cause us to behave in a specific way.

Both parents and teachers of young children commonly use this method of learning. A parent may "time-out" a child who is displaying inappropriate behavior, and a teacher may put a sticker on a child's school assignment that was well done. Punishing the child helps him or her become motivated to behave appropriately; rewarding the child with a sticker for work well done motivates the child to want to do well in school. Either way, this method of modifying behavior can be very successful.

You probably have a lot of personal examples of operant conditioning. Choose one that significantly reinforced a positive behavior and one that significantly reduced a negative behavior.

Positive behavior resulted:

_____

_____

_____

_____

Negative behavior decreased:

_____

_____

_____

_____

ALBERT BANDURA (1925–PRESENT)

Albert Bandura mainly studied aggressive adolescent behavior and theorized that not only does the environment cause specific behaviors, but specific behaviors affect the environment as well. The person's environment and behavior are directly related to one another. Bandura calls this his *social-cognitive personality theory*. "Social" refers to the society in which we live and "cognitive" to how we gather, process, and store information. It is also how we solve problems, think, create, and use language. According to Bandura, cognitive therapy is based on three assumptions:

1. How we feel emotionally and how we behave is directly related to our thoughts.

2. How we perceive (explain what we sense) and how we interpret (understand the meaning) the world and events around us shapes our beliefs and assumptions.

3. If our thoughts are confused, psychological problems could present themselves.

Going one step further, Bandura began to look at the interaction of environment, behavior, and a person's psychological processes, which consist of language and imagination.

Observational Learning or Modeling

Bandura did hundreds of studies, but the "Bobo doll studies" are the most noted and interesting. At the time of these experiments, Bobo the Clown was a very popular circus clown. Bandura had a doll made that resembled Bobo the Clown. Bandura's Bobo was an inflatable oval-shaped balloon doll, weighted in the bottom to allow the doll to pop back up whenever an attempt was made to knock it down.

Bandura hired a young woman to be physically aggressive toward the doll and filmed the woman performing this negative behavior. Bandura showed this film to kindergartners who thought it was funny and seemed to enjoy it a lot. When the film was over and the children returned to the playroom, they saw a Bobo doll exactly like the one in the film. It wasn't a surprise that many of them started to display some of the aggressive behaviors they saw in the film. The interesting fact of this experiment is that the children imitated the woman's behavior without being rewarded. Bandura called this type of learning "modeling," and his theory was called the *social learning theory*.

As young children watch the behaviors of their parents, teachers, idols, and other people within their environment, if they think highly of these individuals, it is a good bet that through modeling they will adopt these behaviors regardless of whether the behaviors are positive or negative.

After studying many examples of modeling, Bandura realized that there were certain steps needed for the modeling process to be successful.

- **Attention:** For an individual to learn anything, he or she needs to pay attention. If something is interesting, the individual is attentive and increased learning occurs; if, however, something is boring, it will be ignored by the individual, thereby decreasing learning.

- **Retention**: Once an individual is paying attention, he or she must remember what is heard.

- **Reproduction**: Now that the individual has paid attention and remembers what was said, he or she must be able to reproduce or reenact the learned behavior.

- **Motivation**: The last step needed for learning through modeling is motivation, a reason for wanting to perform a behavior. The reasons can be positive or negative.

A *positive example* of modeling is when a science teacher demonstrates or models a particular experiment. She is interesting in her presentation and engages her students in the experiment. Because of the positive and interesting way in which she presents the information, the students are able to perform the experiment on their own. They have learned the procedures by modeling their teacher.

A *negative example* is when a father is abusive to his son and often beats him severely for the smallest infractions; the son becomes a bully at school and gets into fights with kids smaller than him, modeling his father's abuse.

What positive behavior have you learned through modeling?

_____
_____
_____
_____

Why is this behavior so memorable to you?

_____
_____
_____
_____

What negative behavior have you learned through modeling?

_____
_____
_____
_____

Why is this behavior so memorable to you—and if you know it is negative, why do you continue to do it?

_____
_____
_____
_____

Positive Motives

Bandura tells us there are three positive motives for controlling our own behavior:

1. Self-observation: Take a good look at yourself and how you behave in society. Be honestly aware of your behavior and how others see you. *Example:* George is going to a job interview and really wants this job. He knows he has the qualifications, but he also knows that first impressions are very important in our society. Consequently, before the interview, George takes the steps necessary to make a good appearance by showering, shaving, neatly combing his hair, and wearing his best suit and tie.

How do you compare yourself to how others see you?

_____
_____
_____
_____

2. Judgment: How does society expect us to behave? What standards are set by society for us, and what standards do we set for ourselves? *Example:* When we are in church, we behave with respect for others and don't yell, shout, curse, or run around wildly. Why? Because society dictates that it is simply unacceptable behavior.

Are you satisfied with how you behave and what others think of your behavior?

_____
_____
_____
_____

I feel my behavior lives up to society's expectations because:

_____
_____
_____
_____

I feel certain parts of my behavior are in conflict with society's expectations, and I can change these behaviors if:

———————————————————————————
———————————————————————————
———————————————————————————
———————————————————————————

3. Self-response: If you compare well with your standards or society's standards, you tend to reward yourself, and if you don't behave appropriately, you tend to punish yourself.

Positive example (reward): Jaime is very conscious about what she eats, and she tries to stay away from sugar and foods that aren't especially nutritious for her. Recently, she put a lot of hard work into studying for her final exams. At the end of her study period, Jaime rewarded herself with a cookie as a special treat.

Negative example (punishment): Gail is very heavy and wants to lose a lot of weight. She has been on a strict diet and doing fairly well. One day at work, someone brought in two dozen doughnuts, and during the workday, Gail ate six of them. When she went home that night, she was disgusted with herself and refused to eat for the rest of the evening. That night, Gail went to bed disappointed and hungry.

What goal did you accomplish, and how did you reward yourself for your success?

———————————————————————————
———————————————————————————
———————————————————————————
———————————————————————————

What was the situation where you disappointed yourself to such a degree that you punished yourself? What was the punishment?

———————————————————————————
———————————————————————————
———————————————————————————
———————————————————————————

If you truly want to improve specific aspects of your life and become a more positive individual, then it is very important for you to practice the exercises you just completed, focusing on those aspects of your behavior you wish to change. Don't forget to also recognize your positive side and consciously reinforce those behaviors. Be honest and gentle with yourself as you continue to go through this process. *You* are the best judge of your character: you know when you are doing well, and you know when you need improvement.

Don't be afraid to talk to yourself and remind yourself that you are a good person and deserve a happier and more positive life. Remember when you focused on your image in the mirror? Do this often and realize that the person looking back at you is your best friend. No one else will ever know you or care about you as much as you should know and care about yourself. Spend some time over the next few months really tuning in to how you talk about yourself. Are you proud of what you do and what you have accomplished, or are you constantly apologizing for your behavior even when it isn't necessary? You may be surprised at what you discover. With practice, you can change negative self-talk into positive self-talk, and when you start to think better of yourself, the people around you will respond in kind.

Remember, you are a work in progress. Take time to become familiar with who you are and what you really want for yourself.

CHAPTER 4

Controlling Your Own Behavior

Now that you have walked with the masters, perhaps one or more of their theories resonates with you more than the others. Take the best of what they have to offer you, and use their concepts and theories to improve your life. We all have room for improvement; you are not alone, and even the most successful individuals in society spend time improving their social behaviors and the image they want to project to society. Remember, first impressions are critical in our society, and no one really wants to listen to a negative person for long.

This is a good time for me to introduce you to journaling; although, that is exactly what you have been doing as you have been working your way through this book. Journaling is a great way for you to see why things happen in your life and whether or not you had control over them. Oftentimes you don't see the immediate effect your behavior had on a situation, and later when reading it in your journal, you see it might have turned out differently had you just handled the situation in a more positive way. As you look back and read what you have written so far, you will see just how revealing writing about yourself and your life experiences can be. Controlling your behavior, especially in emotional situations, can be vital to having a positive outlook on life.

Let's look at how you can control those behaviors you feel are not beneficial in your life. In the space below, write down three of your worst behaviors that you really want to change and why you feel it is necessary for you to change them.

Behavior #1:

_____
_____

I want to change:

_____
_____
_____
_____

Because

_____
_____
_____
_____

Behavior #2:

_____
_____

I want to change:

_____
_____
_____
_____

Because

_____
_____
_____
_____

Behavior #3:

_____
_____

I want to change:

_____
_____
_____
_____

Because

_____
_____
_____
_____

After you have written these behaviors down, review them and choose the one you feel is the most important to improving your outlook on life. Write this behavior in your personal journal. Set yourself some goals and reward yourself when you achieve them. Be conscious of the negative behavior you wish to change, and, in your journal, record your successes but also your failures. Listing your failures will help you to avoid them in the future.

Once you are confident that you have control of this behavior, go on to the next. You will be surprised at how quickly you will become aware of your behavior and how much that behavior impacts your life.

Seeing the Real You

CHAPTER 5

Self-Image

In Part I, you learned how your behaviors affect the way others respond to you and how your negative behavior may keep you from being a positive person. Additionally, you have learned techniques to empower you to adjust personal behaviors that may be keeping you from being successful and content.

The objective of Part II is to help you to understand how you feel about the "real you." Do you see yourself as others see you? Do you see yourself more critically than others around you? Or are you in denial about your inappropriate actions? Do you make excuses for certain behaviors? How do you view the world and your place in it? Do you have high self-esteem or low self-esteem?

It is a normal human desire to be liked and to have others views us in a positive light. Individuals should always strive to maintain good self-esteem (self-image), but often the image they see is negative and depressing. When people feel attractive, worthy, successful, and socially acceptable, their self-esteem is strong. On the other hand, individuals who feel worthless, incompetent, useless, and ugly have low self-esteem; they view the world and their place in it from a very negative perspective. At some time or another, most of us experience moments of both positive and negative self-esteem. However, we each have one view that is more dominant most of the time.

None of us is perfect, but we should choose to work toward perfection even though it is impossible to attain. Why? Striving for perfection allows you to continually improve your self-image by creating a positive attitude that is reinforced through your interactions with others. In turn, this makes you want to improve even more.

As you move forward focusing on your self-image, you will be asked to face various truths about yourself. As the image of who you really are emerges, you will gain a better idea of how you truly see yourself.

Use the same method you used when answering the questions on controlling your behavior. Respond to each question about your self-image with three honest and significant answers. Review them and choose the one you feel needs the most improvement. Write this down in your journal. Use the three positive statements to help you set goals and remember your successes and failures. Don't forget to reward yourself when appropriate. Once you are confident that you have improved that part of your self-image, go on to the next. You will be surprised at how quickly your hard work and positive change in attitude will improve not only how you see yourself, but how others see you as well.

SELF-LIKES VS. SELF-DISLIKES

What are three specific things that you like about yourself? These will be the strengths you use as you work on improving what you dislike.

1. What I like most about myself is:

_____

_____

_____

_____

_____

_____

I feel this way because:

_____

_____

_____

2. What I like most about myself is:

_____

_____

_____

_____

_____

_____

_____

I feel this way because:

_____

_____

_____

_____

3. What I like most about myself is:

_____

_____

_____

_____

_____

_____

_____

I feel this way because:

_____

_____

_____

_____

What are three specific things that you dislike about yourself, and why do you feel this way?

1. What I dislike most about myself is:

_____
_____
_____
_____
_____
_____
_____

I can improve this by:

_____
_____
_____
_____

2. What I dislike most about myself is:

_____
_____
_____
_____
_____
_____
_____
_____

I can improve this by:

_____
_____
_____
_____

3. What I dislike most about myself is:

_____
_____
_____

_____

_____

_____

_____

_____

I can improve this by:

_____

_____

_____

BEST QUALITIES VS. WORST QUALITIES

Some people can easily recognize their positive qualities, while others don't see their greatness because it is overshadowed by a poor self-image. Consider your three best qualities and write them below.

1. One of my best qualities is:

_____

_____

_____

I feel this way because:

_____

_____

_____

2. One of my best qualities is:

_____

_____

_____

I feel this way because:

_____
_____
_____
_____

3. One of my best qualities is:

_____
_____
_____
_____

I feel this way because:

_____
_____
_____
_____

Comparing your best qualities with your worst will reveal your strengths and weaknesses and give you a starting point to change your life for the better. Whenever possible, use your positive qualities to improve what you feel are your worst traits.

1. One of my worst qualities is:

_____
_____
_____
_____

I can improve it by:

_____
_____
_____
_____

2. One of my worst qualities is:

_____

_____

_____

_____

I can improve it by:

_____

_____

_____

_____

3. One of my worst qualities is:

_____

_____

_____

_____

I can improve it by:

_____

_____

_____

_____

ACCOMPLISHMENTS VS. MISTAKES

We all make mistakes; we wouldn't be human if we didn't. However, there are times when we regret our mistakes so much that it overshadows our accomplishments. List your three most successful accomplishments that give you a sense of pride.

1. One of my best accomplishments is:

_____

_____

_____

_____

I feel this way because:

_____
_____
_____
_____

2. One of my best accomplishments is:

_____
_____
_____
_____

I feel this way because:

_____
_____
_____
_____

3. One of my best accomplishments is:

_____
_____
_____
_____

I feel this way because:

_____
_____
_____
_____

We can often forgive ourselves and let go of a troubling situation by analyzing our mistakes. Analyze three of your worst mistakes and describe what you can do in the future to keep from repeating them. As you do this, keep your best accomplishments in mind, for they may be able to help you see a clearer picture of the situation.

1. One of my worst mistakes was:

_____
_____
_____
_____

I can keep from repeating it and work on letting it go by:

_____
_____
_____
_____

2. One of my worst mistakes was:

_____
_____
_____
_____

I can keep from repeating it and work on letting it go by:

_____
_____
_____
_____

3. One of my worst mistakes was:

_____
_____
_____
_____

I can keep from repeating it and work on letting it go by:

_____
_____
_____
_____

Interesting vs. Boring

There are times when you are with a group of people who find you very interesting, and there are times when it is obvious that people are ignoring you. It is practically impossible to be interesting every time a social situation arises. However, by focusing on the times you absolutely know you were a bore, you can prevent future embarrassment. This exercise will help you recognize the interesting parts of your personality and find a solution that will keep the boring parts from appearing at the worst possible times. List three personality traits that you positively know make you interesting when talking with others.

1. One of my more interesting traits is:

_____

_____

_____

_____

I feel this way because:

_____

_____

_____

2. One of my more interesting traits is:

_____

_____

_____

_____

I feel this way because:

_____

_____

_____

3. One of my more interesting traits is:

_____
_____
_____
_____

I feel this way because:

_____
_____
_____
_____

Think of all the interesting aspects of your personality. How can you use them to recognize when you are starting to become boring? Knowing this can help you to stop before embarrassing yourself.

1. One of my more boring traits is:

_____
_____
_____
_____

I can recognize this trait before embarrassing myself by:

_____
_____
_____
_____

2. One of my more boring traits is:

_____
_____
_____
_____

I can recognize this trait before embarrassing myself by:

_____

_____

_____

_____

3. One of my more boring traits is:

_____

_____

_____

_____

I can recognize this trait before embarrassing myself by:

_____

_____

_____

_____

HARDWORKING VS. LAZY

Do you consider yourself a hardworking person? Or do you view yourself as being lazy most of the time? Hard work takes motivation and effort, and it is one the most important parts of personal success. I don't know of any successful lazy people! Consider three of the most memorable times when you were a hardworking individual. What was the positive result of that hard work?

1. A time when my hard work ended with positive results is:

_____

_____

_____

_____

I was motivated to do this work because:

_____

_____

_____

_____

2. A time when my hard work ended with positive results is:

_____

_____

_____

_____

I was motivated to do this work because:

_____

_____

_____

_____

3. A time when my hard work ended with positive results is:

_____

_____

_____

_____

I was motivated to do this work because:

_____

_____

_____

_____

Laziness can be overcome with motivation. That is why I have had you list the times you put your best effort into a project or situation. List three of the most memorable times when you failed to be successful because you were just downright lazy. How can the positive result of your hard work motivate you in the future when a lazy mood strikes you?

1. A time when my laziness led to negative results is:

_____
_____
_____
_____

The motivation that I could have used to change it is:

_____
_____
_____
_____

2. A time when my laziness led to negative results is:

_____
_____
_____
_____

The motivation that I could have used to change it is:

_____
_____
_____
_____

3. A time when my laziness led to negative results is:

_____
_____
_____
_____

The motivation that I could have used to change it is:

_____
_____
_____
_____

CREATIVE MIND VS. SLEEPING MIND

Creativity is something that comes easy to some people, while others have to work at it. One thing you can bet on is that we have all been given creative talents, but often these talents are latent (asleep) or go unnoticed. We have all had creative moments, but some individuals don't believe this because they haven't taken the time to recognize their creative accomplishments. Now is the time for you to recognize yours. List below three of your most creative accomplishments and how you felt when they were achieved.

1. One of my most memorable creative accomplishments is:

_____

_____

_____

_____

Upon completion of this accomplishment, I felt:

_____

_____

_____

_____

2. One of my most memorable creative accomplishments is:

_____

_____

_____

_____

Upon completion of this accomplishment, I felt:

_____

_____

_____

_____

3. One of my most memorable creative accomplishments is:

_____

_____

_____

_____

Upon completion of this accomplishment, I felt:

_____

_____

_____

_____

If you have rarely experienced a creative thought, it is time to stretch your mind. The mind is like a muscle; it needs to be exercised to be more productive. In order to spark creativity, we have to make the effort to consciously think about our talents and how those talents could benefit us. Then we have to take a leap of faith and go for it! Think of three important times when you didn't attempt a project or task because you felt you didn't have the creativity to do it. What would have motivated you to wake up your creativity and take a stab at the project or task?

1. One important project or task I didn't attempt to do is:

_____

_____

_____

_____

Looking back, I could have been motivated to do it if:

_____

_____

_____

_____

2. One important project or task I didn't attempt to do is:

_____
_____
_____
_____

Looking back, I could have been motivated to do it if:

_____
_____
_____
_____

3. One important project or task I didn't attempt to do is:

_____
_____
_____
_____

Looking back, I could have been motivated to do it if:

Right Decisions vs. Wrong Decisions

Decisions, decisions: they are a major part of our daily life. You don't always make the right decisions? Well, welcome to the human race! We have all made bad decisions we have lived to regret. What is important is to recognize why you made the wrong decision and how you can avoid doing so in the future. The best way is to look at the times when you made some very positive decisions that had a great effect on your life. Next, determine what was different in those situations that caused you to make the right choice. Let's start with listing three of the best decisions you made that resulted in a positive outcome and why you chose to make that particular decision.

1. One of the best decisions I have ever made is:

_____
_____
_____
_____

I made this decision because:

_____

_____

_____

_____

2. One of the best decisions I have ever made is:

_____

_____

_____

_____

I made this decision because:

_____

_____

_____

_____

3. One of the best decisions I have ever made is:

_____

_____

_____

_____

I made this decision because:

_____

_____

_____

_____

It's not good to dwell on the poor decisions we have made, but it is a good idea to look at them objectively. By understanding why these decisions were made, we can prevent ourselves from repeating them in the future. So what were three of the worst decisions you have made in your life, and what can you do to avoid making them in the future?

1. One of the worst decisions I have ever made is:

_____

_____

_____

_____

I can avoid making the same decision in the future by:

_____

_____

_____

_____

2. One of the worst decisions I have ever made is:

_____

_____

_____

_____

I can avoid making the same decision in the future by:

_____

_____

_____

_____

3. One of the worst decisions I have ever made is:

_____

_____

_____

_____

I can avoid making the same decision in the future by:

_____

_____

_____

_____

Good Attitude vs. Bad Attitude

How you view the world is a matter of your attitude. With a good attitude, you can overcome the many hurdles that life throws at you. However, a bad attitude can only make your life more difficult. What are three specific times things may have gone very badly if it weren't for your positive attitude? What was different about these situations that helped you to be positive?

1. A time when my positive attitude saved me from a bad situation was:

_____

_____

_____

I chose to be positive because:

_____

_____

_____

2. A time when my positive attitude saved me from a bad situation was:

_____

_____

_____

_____

I chose to be positive because:

_____

_____

_____

3. A time when my positive attitude saved me from a bad situation was:

_____
_____
_____
_____

I chose to be positive because:

_____
_____
_____
_____

It can feel as though our society views the world through negative eyes by focusing on the hopelessness of war, poverty, and suffering rather than intervening in a positive way to make it better. Unfortunately, this makes it very difficult for us to always have a positive attitude. However, if you really want to be content and strive for happiness in your life, then you must move forward with a positive attitude. No one ever attains these goals by being negative, and if this is how you have been seeing your life, it is definitely time for a major change. List three specific situations where your bad attitude got you in trouble. How could you have changed your attitude and prevented the situation?

1. A time when my negative attitude got me in trouble was:

_____
_____
_____
_____

A positive attitude may have changed the outcome by:

_____
_____
_____
_____

2. A time when my negative attitude got me in trouble was:

_____
_____
_____
_____

A positive attitude may have changed the outcome by:

_____
_____
_____
_____

3. A time when my negative attitude got me in trouble was:

_____
_____
_____
_____

A positive attitude may have changed the outcome by:

_____
_____
_____
_____

There are so many facets to a person's self-image and so many factors that affect a person's self-esteem. The exercises you have completed barely scratch the surface. However, having completed them, you can now focus on the specific aspects of your personality that you can work on to improve your self-esteem.

Without judgment, in the space below, list those qualities that you feel are preventing you from feeling good about yourself.

Now start working on improving them one at a time. Use your journal to set reasonable, reachable goals and to keep track of your results. Don't forget to give yourself a reward when you have earned one.

I hope you are still with me and ready to embark on the last leg of your journey. Moving forward, we will discuss our emotional self and how our emotions drive all of the decisions we make.

Part III

Emotions Are the Driving Force

CHAPTER 6

Making Emotional Choices

Everything we have discussed to this point has been driven by human emotions. The spark that ignites the emotions (stimulus) may produce an immediate reaction (response) to the situation. This immediate reaction may or may not produce a positive outcome, depending on what has caused the situation. Additionally, one doesn't always think clearly when reacting emotionally to a person or situation. Therefore, it is imperative that we remember to stop and think before we react. How many times have you heard the phrases "think before you speak" or "count to ten before you react"? These phrases stem from mistakes individuals have made throughout human history that sprang from an emotional reaction rather than rational thought.

Human emotions, whether positive or negative, are psychological warnings that something is about happen. A wise person listens to these warnings, considers the situation, and takes the time to act appropriately rather than simply reacting. An age-old example is a teenage boy and girl who have been dating for several months, and their emotions and physical desires are becoming overwhelming. They truly believe they are "in love," and they react to this emotion by engaging their physical desires without considering the possible outcome. A few months later, the girl discovers she is pregnant, and a whole new set of emotions comes into play. If these teens had taken the time to calm their emotions and consider the possible outcome of their actions, they could have prevented a pregnancy for which they were not prepared. All emotions have an opposite, and it is important to recognize the options before deciding upon your actions. By doing so, you could possibly prevent a life-altering outcome. The goal of the following exercise is to help you understand your emotions and realize that you have options when making emotional decisions.

In the previous exercises, you either responded to a specific question or answered the question by choosing three personal life experiences. Since your emotions play such a major role in your life, the following exercises will be more specific to the emotions being discussed. I will ask you to choose the one most significant situation you can remember that affected your life in a major way. What follows is a series of guided questions to help you analyze the situation from a different perspective.

As you review the choices you have made, you will better understand them, regardless of whether the outcome was positive or negative. You will see what caused you to make those choices and, if the outcome was not so great, what you could have done to avoid it. No one is perfect, and we have all made irrational and emotional decisions in life. Be truthful with your responses but also nonjudgmental with yourself. This exercise is not a "magic pill" that will protect you from ever making emotional mistakes in the future. However, it should help to reduce how often they occur. Let's begin.

ANGER VS. PATIENCE

Anger is a passionate display of extreme displeasure. When we are angry, especially with another person, it is very difficult to think clearly and react well.

It is important to remember that when you allow your anger to rule your behavior and you lash out at the person you are angry with, you give away your power. Think about this for a minute. If your immediate reaction to anger is to retaliate, you are allowing this emotion to weaken you. This might cause you to make the wrong choice. In doing this, you have given the person you are angry at the power to derail you and send you in the wrong direction. Think of a time in your life you regret, when you were so angry and out of control that the situation ended very badly. Then answer the following questions truthfully.

Describe a situation you regret, where you wish you had been able to control your anger:

_____
_____
_____
_____
_____
_____
_____
_____
_____
_____
_____

Why were you unable to control your anger?

_____
_____
_____
_____

What was the result of your anger?

_____
_____
_____
_____

Was there anything you could have done to prevent your anger from getting out of control?

_____
_____
_____
_____

Patience gives you the ability to deal with a situation, no matter how painful or difficult it may be. When you take the time to think through a situation and make a conscious choice that is not based on an emotional reaction, the chances of making the right choice are greatly improved. Having patience in an angry situation doesn't mean you should allow the other individual to cause you any harm. What patience will do is prevent you from causing yourself harm. This doesn't mean you have to take a long time to think through the situation at hand. When you practice patience, you can call upon it at a moment's notice. This can give you the power to make a decision that may save you from disastrous consequences.

Describe a time when you displayed extreme patience and consciously controlled your anger:

_____
_____
_____
_____
_____
_____
_____
_____
_____
_____

What happened that allowed you to have patience?

_____
_____
_____
_____

How did you benefit yourself and others by having patience?

_____
_____
_____
_____

What could have happened at that time if you had not had patience?

_____

_____

_____

_____

WORRY VS. CONFIDENCE

Worry is an uneasy feeling that results when you feel threatened by a person, place, or situation. We all seem to worry too much. Most of us worry about things that we cannot control, things that may never happen. Worrying creates a negative place from which a positive solution is hard to see. You are less likely to take a positive action, whether to find a solution or simply to summon the strength to accept it.

Describe a time when you were overwhelmed with worry:

_____

_____

_____

_____

_____

_____

_____

_____

_____

_____

Did your worrying help the situation?

_____

_____

_____

_____

How did your worrying affect those around you (family, friends)?

_____

_____

_____

_____

Looking back on the situation, if you had been able to control your worrying, could the outcome have been better?

_____

_____

_____

_____

Confidence is a belief in yourself and your abilities. Confidence gives you the ability to see a stressful situation from a position of strength and hope. It places you in a positive frame of mind, enabling you to take charge. When life seems to be overwhelming and it feels like everything is going wrong, you have two options: worry about it, or have the confidence to do something about it.

Describe a situation where you could have worried, but having confidence allowed you to resolve the situation in a positive way:

_____

_____

_____

_____

_____

_____

_____

_____

_____

_____

Why were you able to be confident in this situation, but not in the one above?

_____

_____

_____

_____

How did those involved benefit from your confidence and positive attitude?

_____

_____

_____

_____

Looking back on the situation, what could have happened if you didn't take confident and positive action?

_____

_____

_____

_____

FEAR VS. FAITH

Fear is an intense sense of impending danger. We have all experienced that horrible feeling in the pit of our stomachs when we think something awful is going to happen. Fear can also be so irrational and overwhelming that it blinds you from taking positive steps to resolve it.

Describe a situation where you were so paralyzed with fear that you could not see a positive solution:

_____

_____

_____

_____

_____

_____

What caused you to be so terrified by this fear that you couldn't handle it?

_____

_____

_____

_____

What was the end result in this fearful situation?

_____

_____

_____

_____

Looking back on the situation, was there anything you or someone else could have done to ease your fear?

_____

_____

_____

_____

Faith is the ability to trust yourself in a fearful situation, knowing that you have the ability to survive it. It is your ability to see a fearful situation from a rational perspective. Although faith involves knowing that others in your life are willing to help you in tough times, the person you _must_ always have faith in is yourself. By facing your fears, you lessen their power over you and put them in the proper perspective.

What is the most memorable time that having faith in a fearful situation saved you?

_____

_____

_____

_____

What specific factor allowed your faith to overcome your fear?

_____

_____

_____

_____

How did overcoming this fear affect you and others?

_____

_____

_____

_____

What could have happened if you didn't have enough faith in yourself to resolve the fearful situation?

_____

_____

_____

_____

SELFISHNESS VS. GENEROSITY

Selfishness is caring only about things that will benefit you. If this is how you see yourself, you are missing out on all the wonderful rewards that come with giving to others. Selfish people generally experience a false sense of satisfaction when their needs are met, but in reality they usually find themselves alone when they are the ones who need help.

Describe a situation where you were regrettably selfish:

_____

_____

_____

_____

_____

_____

_____

What about this situation prevented you from controlling your selfishness?

_____
_____
_____
_____

What was the result of your being selfish? Were others hurt because of you?

_____
_____
_____
_____

Was there anything you could have done to prevent your selfishness from getting out of control?

_____
_____
_____
_____

Generosity is when you give of yourself without expecting anything in return. In other words, you put others' needs above your own. By giving of yourself, you open the door to receive when the situation is reversed and you need another person's generosity.

Describe a situation where you feel you were particularly generous:

_____
_____
_____
_____
_____
_____
_____
_____
_____

What happened that caused you to be so generous?

_____
_____
_____
_____

How did you and those involved benefit from your generosity?

_____
_____
_____
_____

What could have happened if you had chosen not to be generous?

_____
_____
_____
_____

CRITICISM VS. SYMPATHY

Criticism is passing judgment on the merits of others. If you tend to be critical, have you considered the effect your words and actions have on others? Often the person you are criticizing is merely acting as a mirror to reflect your own image of yourself. Therefore, the person you are really criticizing is yourself! Criticism is a very negative emotion, and it almost never ends well. On rare occasions, "constructive criticism" can be beneficial if given in a positive way, but even then it may turn out badly.

Describe a specific situation where you were especially critical of another person:

_____
_____
_____
_____
_____
_____

What about this situation caused you to be so critical?

_____

_____

_____

_____

What resulted from your being so judgmental? Did someone else get hurt?

_____

_____

_____

_____

What could you have done to be less critical in that situation?

_____

_____

_____

_____

Sympathy is a relationship between individuals where the situation of one produces a compassionate response in another. The supportive words of a sympathetic person can often be just what are needed to turn someone else's life in a more positive direction. A sympathetic word or action can make all the difference.

Describe a situation where you were very sympathetic:

_____

_____

_____

_____

_____

_____

_____

_____

_____

Why did you feel so sympathetic with this individual?

_____

_____

_____

_____

How did your sympathy and compassion help the other person?

_____

_____

_____

_____

What could have happened if you had chosen not to be sympathetic?

_____

_____

_____

_____

DISHONESTY VS. COURAGE

Dishonesty is when people pretend to have character, values, and morals, but in reality they do not. Rather, dishonest people fulfill their own needs through lying, cheating, and unfairly profiting from others. Dishonest people use others to succeed because it is easier than working hard for true success. These individuals are often called scam artists, and many have become extremely wealthy by abusing others. We may not have gone to the lengths of the scam artists, but I can assure you that we have all been dishonest at one time or another in our lives. Use the space below to write about one incident where you were dishonest.

Describe a memorable time when you were dishonest:

_____

_____

_____

_____

Why were you dishonest in this situation?

_____

_____

_____

_____

What was the result of your dishonesty? Were others hurt because of you?

_____

_____

_____

_____

Was there anything you could have done to prevent yourself from being dishonest?

_____

_____

_____

_____

Courage is the ability to face difficulties with bravery and a sense of pride in personal actions. Courageous people aren't afraid to work hard for something they want to achieve. When their lives get difficult, they don't use others to make their situation easier. Instead, they focus on their own strengths to help them overcome their difficulties. When morals, pride, and bravery encompass all aspects of your life, you can face your own difficulties with courage.

What difficult situation were you able to overcome by being courageous?

_____

_____

_____

_____

What was different about this situation that you chose to face it with courage?

_____

_____

_____

_____

What was the result of your being courageous, and what might have happened if you had not been?

_____

_____

_____

_____

What can you take from that situation that will be useful in the future when you need to have courage again?

_____

_____

_____

_____

Prejudice vs. Forgiveness

Prejudice is an unfavorable opinion formed without prior knowledge, thought, or reason. Prejudice is often a learned emotion passed on from generation to generation. Those who feel they are a victim of prejudice usually return it with a prejudice of their own, continuing the cycle.

What specific situation was so intense that it resulted in your being prejudiced?

_____

_____

_____

_____

Why couldn't you control your prejudice?

_____

_____

_____

_____

What was the result of your prejudice, and were others involved?

_____

_____

_____

_____

Was there anything you could have done to prevent yourself from being prejudiced?

_____

_____

_____

_____

Forgiveness is the willingness to stop resenting another individual or group. Forgiveness plays a major role in countering prejudice. We must realize that those who show prejudice toward us are reacting out of fear from false information they have learned. In order to stop prejudice, we must be willing to forgive those who are prejudiced against us. Only then can we end the cycle of hatred and fear.

Describe a specific situation where you showed amazing forgiveness:

_____

_____

_____

_____

_____

_____

_____

_____

Why were you able to be so forgiving?

_____

_____

_____

_____

How did you and those involved benefit from your forgiveness?

_____

_____

_____

_____

What might have happened if you hadn't been so forgiving?

_____

_____

_____

_____

JEALOUSY VS. RESPONSIBILITY

Jealousy is mental uneasiness from fear of rivalry. People who are jealous are afraid that others will get ahead of them and steal their success. They are so busy being jealous that they prevent themselves from advancing and becoming successful in their own right. Without ethical consideration, jealous people often do whatever it takes to outdo those who have made them jealous. Ultimately, jealousy blinds them to the truth and to positive opportunities that may come their way. It is part of human nature to be jealous, but hopefully you haven't let it go too far.

Describe a situation where you were extremely jealous:

_____

_____

_____

_____

_____

Why were you so jealous?

_____

_____

_____

_____

How did your jealousy affect you and those involved?

_____

_____

_____

_____

Was there anything you could have done to prevent your jealousy from getting out of control?

_____

_____

_____

_____

Responsibility is the obligation to do what is morally right. We should behave responsibly in business, at school, and with our friends and family. The responsibility to do the right thing is always present. Deep inside each of us is a voice that has been telling us since early childhood what is right and wrong. Responsible people succeed in many of their endeavors because they approach them with confidence rather than jealousy.

Describe a situation where you were very responsible:

_____

_____

_____

_____

_____

_____

_____

_____

What made you feel a sense of responsibility?

_____
_____
_____
_____

How did your being responsible affect yourself and others?

_____
_____
_____
_____

Can you remember anything about this situation that could help you avoid becoming jealous in the future?

_____
_____
_____
_____

HATE VS. LOVE

Hate is a passionate dislike of a person, place, situation, or object. We tend to hate so many things. People hate their jobs, students hate school, people hate one another, and entire countries hate other countries. There seems to be so much hatred in the world that it's no wonder many people view life as difficult and negative. When hate is taken to an extreme, it causes war, poverty, and despair.

What specific situation caused you to feel hatred or at least a strong dislike for a person or situation?

_____
_____
_____
_____
_____
_____
_____

_____

_____

_____

_____

_____

Why did you feel so much hatred?

_____

_____

_____

_____

How did your hatred affect you and others involved?

_____

_____

_____

_____

Was there anything you could have done to prevent your hatred from getting out of control?

_____

_____

_____

_____

Love is a strong or passionate affection for a person, situation, or thing. A very good way to overcome hatred is with love and compassion. What we hate is never all bad. With compassion, there is always something we can find to love or understand even just a little bit. When we approach what we hate with compassion and understanding, the most difficult situations become much easier. If our civilization is going to survive, we must start becoming more compassionate and loving toward each other.

Describe a situation where you were extremely compassionate and loving:

_____

_____

_____

_____

_____

_____

_____

_____

_____

_____

_____

What sparked your compassion and love?

_____

_____

_____

_____

How did your compassion and love affect you and those involved?

_____

_____

_____

_____

What can you remember that will help you be more compassionate in the future if you find yourself feeling hateful?

_____

_____

_____

_____

Putting the New Pieces Together

At the beginning of the book, I asked you to look at your image in a mirror and write down in the frame everything you felt about what you saw. I then asked you to write a short autobiography of how you saw your life in that moment. Now that you have completed the workbook, I would like you to repeat these two activities and then compare them. Write down in the frame below the similarities and differences as you analyze them. Use your journal to comment on your results. Have you found a dramatic difference, somewhat of a difference, or no difference at all?

On the next page, write about your future life, and include all the positive opportunities that you never knew you had!

THIS WILL BE MY LIFE

_____

_____

_____

_____

_____

_____

_____

_____

_____

_____

_____

_____

_____

_____

_____

_____

_____

_____

_____

_____

_____

_____

_____

_____

_____

_____

_____

_____

_____

_____

_____

_____

Conclusion

This book describes only a few of the emotions that control our behaviors and our lives. The opposites of each emotion given are ones that seemed reasonable to me. You can surely find differing opinions if you choose to research them. If you see them differently, that's okay. What's important to understand is that people, places, and situations can be viewed both negatively and positively.

Through these exercises, I hope you have come to know yourself more honestly. Now that you are using your personal journal, you can choose to focus on any section of this book that seems to affect your life at a given time. These tools can improve your life dramatically, especially if there is something you want to change about yourself.

When life throws you a curveball, and you are unsure how to respond, use this journal to write down the possible positive or negative approaches to your situation. Analyze both, and hopefully you will be able to make the decision that is best for you. I bet you will choose the positive over the negative nine times out of ten.

Please remember that completing this workbook one time does not mean that you no longer have to focus on the exercises presented. This book is intended to be used frequently. By reading over the material, the questions, and your responses again, you can spin off from this book to continue working in your journal. In time, you can greatly improve the parts of your personality and behavior that keep you from being positive and content with your life.

I hope you have enjoyed your journey of self-discovery. It is probably the most important journey you will ever make. I encourage you to practice daily the lessons you have learned and to keep a journal of your experiences.

Journaling is a wonderful way to see improvement and keep you moving in a positive direction.

I am proud of you for taking the time to finish this workbook and for completing the questions and activities with honesty and integrity. It is definitely not an easy thing to do. In addition, as you continue your journey, remember not to be too critical of your mistakes. Rather, analyze them to find out what caused you to make them and to discover what positive messages you can take away from them. You only have one life to live, and you can live it to its fullest! You can choose to be as happy, successful, and content as possible. The only way this will happen is if you take the time to think about your needs and goals as well as the positive ways in which you can pursue them. Time is important, but not as important as you! You're worth the effort!

Always remember to "keep your glass half full." Have a wonderful life!

References

Following are the websites the author used to research the material included in this publication. To site each individual publication would have required an additional book.

http://psychology.about.com/od/psychology101/u/psychology-theories.htm#s1
http://en.wikipedia.org/wiki/Psychology
http://www.bbc.co.uk/science/humanbody/mind/articles/psychology/what_is_psychology.shtml
http://www.apa.org/helpcenter/about-psychologists.aspx
http://psychology.about.com/od/classicalconditioning/a/pavlovs-dogs.htm
http://lightworker.com/VirtualLight/BookReviews/?p=30
http://www.raysofdawn.com/Testimonials.cfm
http://en.wikipedia.org/wiki/Sigmund_Freud
http://psychology.about.com/od/sigmundfreud/p/sigmund_freud.htm
http://webspace.ship.edu/cgboer/freud.html
http://www.brainyquote.com/quotes/authors/s/sigmund_freud.html
http://www.law.uchicago.edu/files/files/20.Sykes_.Regression.pdf
http://psychology.about.com/library/bl_psychosocial_summary.htm
http://en.wikipedia.org/wiki/B._F._Skinner
http://webspace.ship.edu/cgboer/bandura.html
http://www.mindtools.com/pages/article/newTED_91.htm
http://www.emotionsanonymous.org/
http://en.wikipedia.org/wiki/Anger
http://www.squidoo.com/howtostopbeinglazy
http://www.time.com/time/magazine/article/0,9171,1147152,00.html
http://newthoughtlibrary.com/holmesErnest/CreativeMindAndSuccess/cmas_003.htm#TopOfText
http://en.wikipedia.org/wiki/Introspection
http://www.alleydog.com/glossary/definition.php?term=Introspection
http://www.goodreads.com/quotes/tag/introspection
http://www.vocabulary.com/dictionary/accomplishment
http://en.wikipedia.org/wiki/Attitude_%28psychology%29
http://en.wikipedia.org/wiki/Human_behavior
https://www.concept-therapy.org/product-details.cfm?PID=3&WPID=1